NBK22912

Published and printed in The United States of America

www.newalbanybooks.com

1939-1954
Includes Suburban, Rambler, Metropolitan, Nash-Healey

By
Don Narus

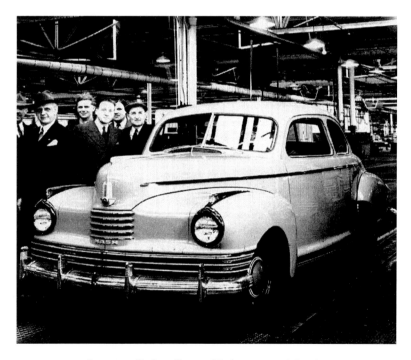

Last off the line, February 1942

www.newalbanybooks.com

You're Going to Like This

If you have any expectation that you know what a Nash "600" is like—stop right here.

You may know that it delivers 25 to 30 miles on a gallon of gasoline, at moderate highway speeds—(and that's wonderful).

You may know that it's just as big inside as it looks outside—that the front seat is divan size, and the back seat can be turned into a soft double bed at night. That's swell, too.

And you have heard about the Nash Weather-Eye Conditioned Air System that furnishes fresh, filtered, air—warm as you dial it—without dust or drafts. And that's *something*.

But this is what you can't know—until you *drive* a Nash "600"—

Here is something so brand-new in performance that it adds up to a new type of automobile. It steers, parks, handles easier —it is amazingly quiet—and with deep coil springs on all four wheels you can really g-l-i-d-e over rough roads.

The old-time drag of extra weight— that's out. The rattles and squeaks of bolted construction—they're gone! Instead, in a Nash "600," body and frame

are one welded steel unit—clean, trim and husky as a B-29!

It's a new kind of motoring, made possible by a *new* kind of car. And the price? You're going to like that, too; it's in the low-price field.

Do it—drive a new Nash "600." Your dealer has it, along with the new Nash Ambassador. See him today.

. . .

Tune in the Nash-Kelvinator Musical Hit— David Rose and his Orchestra with Curt Massey. Wednesdays 10:30 p.m., Eastern Daylight Time. Columbia Broadcasting System.

NASH MOTORS · Division of Nash-Kelvinator Corporation, Detroit, Michigan

YOU'LL BE AHEAD WITH *Nash*

4

Contents

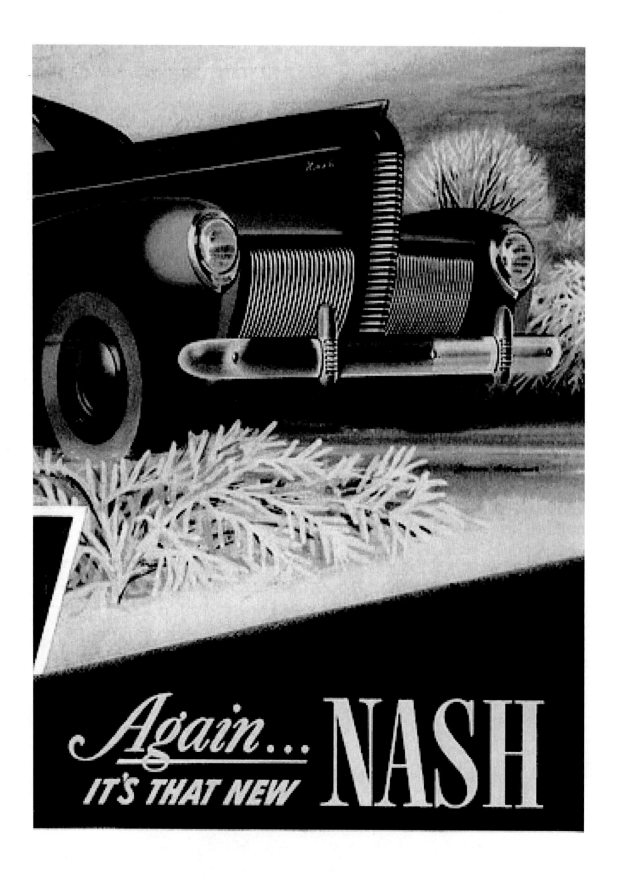

Nash

1939-1954
By
Don Narus

Printed on Premium White in the United States of America by LuLu Press, Raleigh, NC. Type set in Arial. No part of this work may be duplicated or transferred electronically or reproduced in any format without the consent of the author, with the exception of written book reviews. Quotes and text excerpts are allowed with reference and or credit given to this work or the author. Copies of this book may be purchased directly from the publisher, New Albany Books.

ISBN 978-1-4675-2124-6

Copyright 2012 Donald Narus

Published by
New Albany Books
2523 Pine Ridge Way S. B-1, Palm Harbor, Florida 34684

First Edition
0123456789

Narus, Donald J. (Don)
  1.Nash, 2. Nash 600, 3.Nash Lafayette 4.Nash woodie, 5. Nash Suburban. 6.Nash Ambassador, 7. Nash Post-War Cars

www.newalbanybooks.com

Credits and Acknowledgments

Thanks to the following for making this book possible: Photo credits: photos were obtained from various sources including the internet. Yahoo.com Images, Flickr.Com, Conceptcarz.com., Wikipedia.com, Oldcarsandtruckpictures.com, Auto-lit.com, featuredcars.com, Steve Brown/ejb4photos, Patrick Schilling, John MacDonald, Bruce Barnett, Sfastnov Cestu, A&E Classics, John Trotta, Jim Fliter. Jim List, Eric Nelson Jr., Earl Brancolino, RexGray / flickr.com, Nash Car Club of America, Metropolitan Nash Club of America. Every effort was made to identify the photo and photographer, some were readily available while others were not; thanks to all those who we could not readily identify.

Publishers Note: The images reproduced in this book are digital, from download digital images of various sizes. Some are originally black and white (factory photos) most others are color converted to black and white. While all images were necessary to the content of this book their quality varies. The best images available of the examples shown were chosen. Every attempt was made to obtain the sharpest images. If better images become available they will be used in revised editions.

Special Thanks: To John Slusar, my good friend and Chief Editor, who always keeps me on track. We share a love of cars, books and the written word.
To Jim Bracewell, my Content Editor. Your willingness to help and contribute is greatly appreciated.   Thank you gentlemen.

Cover photos
Front cover: Saturday Evening Post Ad March, 1947, Howard Scott artist

Back cover: Newsweek Ad, July, 1950

Introduction

Charles W. Nash resigned as President of General Motors in 1916 to form his own car company. He acquired the Thomas B. Jeffery Company of Kenosha, Wisconsin, and renamed it Nash Motors. The first Nash debuted in 1917 as the model 671. In 1924 Nash purchased LaFeyette Motors. Sales were good and Nash found itself in eighth place during the 1920s.

In the market crash of 1929, Nash was in jeopardy, but it struggled along. In 1934 Nash built its millionth car and introduced the new entry level 400 series. In order to strenghten it's financial position Nash merged with the Kelvinator Appliance Company in 1937. The name was changed to: Nash-Kalvinator. George Mason continued as President, while Charles Nash became Chairman of the Board.

Charles Nash believed in value. A Nash gave you a lot for the money and the cars came with many new innovations. For example: the "The Twin Ignition Eight", cowl ventilation, the dashboard starter button (instead of the industry standard floor starter), shatter-proof safety glass, radiator vents, downdraft carburetors, "Syncro-Safety Shift" and free wheeling. All of these features were standard in the high-end models, but many were found in the entry level Nash.

In 1938 Nash-Kelvinator sales dropped due to a recession that hurt the auto industry in general. Nash was due for a much needed face lift. That year it introduced the "Weather-Eye" heating/ventilating system, which would become the best system in the industry for the next 20 years.

A totally new car was offered for 1939 with fender interrogated headlamps and a stacked narrow horizontal bar grille with vertical bars on either side. The design was considered *"Art-Deco"*. The LaFayette, introduced as the low priced entry in 1937, was the best seller. Although the company lost money (over $1 million in 1939) its future looked bright. By 1940 Nash-Kelvinator had once again become profitable, and produced over 62,000 cars.

HOW MUCH *Excitement* CAN YOU STAND?

IT'S SAFE to hunt thrills—in a Nash! New wider windshield assures perfect vision . . . extra big hydraulic brakes stop at split-moment notice. Even the steering is surer, safer!

AHEAD OF TIME—new lively Nash engine whips through traffic, flashes from 15 to 50 MPH, in 13 seconds, in high.

NO MATTER where you've taken your fun—as the anchor man on an Alpine climb or in the saddle of a thoroughbred . . .

You're going to find a new tingle in your pulse when you drive this new Nash.

Here it is, waiting for your inspection now. A long silver bullet of a car . . . poised for instant flight—*it looks alive!*

And it IS alive . . . all it needs is you to let it loose. But—go easy —*it's fire on four wheels!*

Try to keep that whistle off your lips when that new power-packed engine lets go . . . when that Fourth Speed Forward* sends you bursting into a new range of performance.

Just try to be bored when you discover that you can take the lead over the pack, on hill or flat, and never hear your engine.

Try to be blasé when a tiny dial you twirl brings fresh-conditioned air to keep out dust and drafts and banish chilly moments.

Try to look indifferent when you cruise down a busy street and find yourself the center of attention.

Then try to go back to quiet ways and ordinary automobiles!

Sounds exciting, but here's still more . . . you'll find a new Steering Post Shift* . . . soundproofing that lets you drive all day in perfect relaxation . . . and sedans have a convertible bed for that vacation trip.

Ten models are priced next to the lowest! So get a Nash from your dealer—and *try* to keep calm.

Four Series of Great Cars. 22 Models . . . 10 Priced Next to the Lowest . . . Delivered at Factory, as Low as $770. Stand. Equipment and Federal Taxes Incl. **$770**

(*Optional Equipment—Slight Extra Charge*)

Convertible Coupe, 117-inch Wheelbase, is $959 delivered at factory, with Standard equipment and federal taxes included. (White sidewall tires and rear wheel-shields are optional at extra cost.) 1800 Dealers from Maine to California to serve you. NASH MOTORS DIVISION, Nash-Kelvinator Corporation, Detroit, Michigan.

NEW ENGINE development betters '38 gas economy by 10%, lets you do the usual day's touring on a tankful.

It's that New NASH
THE CAR EVERYBODY LIKES

Chapter One
1939-1940

In 1938 Nash Motors, along with the rest of the auto industry, was hurt by an economic recession. Sales were nearly cut in half of those for 1937. Only 41,543 cars were produced for the year which translated to a loss of over $7 million dollars. The only noteworthy innovation from Nash for 1938, was the introduction of the "Weather-Eye" heating and ventilation system. It would remain one of the best from Detroit for the next 20 years.

Undeterred by the poor showing of 1938, Nash Motors President George Mason ordered a complete redesign for 1939. A redesigned front end featured flush fit headlamps and waterfall accents astride a vertical tower of horizontal bars. The total design incorporated the best of the *"Art Deco"* period. Sales rebounded sharply and production reached 63,000 units overall with 49,312 for the model year. The LaFayette accounted for close to 50 percent.

Three series were offered for 1939: the entry level LaFayette with a 117 inch wheelbase, the median Ambassador Six with a 121 inch wheelbase and top of the line, larger, Ambassador Eight with a 125 inch wheelbase. Within the series, LaFayette had ten models, while the Ambassador Six and Eight series, had six models each. There were two style types of sedans available: the *"Trunk Back"*, which was more traditional and the *"Slipstream"*, a new streamlined *Fastback.* The *Trunk Back* outsold the *Fastback,* as buyers stuck to the traditional design.

Nash had survived the 1938 recession. Revenue for 1939 amounted to $72,534,000. with a total loss of $1.6 million, as compared to a loss of $7.6 million for 1938. Nash was well on its way to a full recovery. Things were looking up.

For 1940, Nash continued to promote its innovative features, claiming, *"The Most Modern Car in the World."* Ambassador Sixes and Eights featured *"Twin Ignition"* inline engines. There were two spark plugs for each cylinder. Mandated by the government in transport planes, it was only available in the Nash and Rolls-Royce.

Convertibles offered fold down *"Opera Seats"*, for two additional passengers also available in *All-Purpose* Coupes. The clutch starter was another unique feature. Depress the clutch down to the floor to start the car.

Interiors were advertised as having *"soft, billowy seats. More comfortable than your favorite arm chair."* The dashboard was wood grained with chrome accents. Instrument gauges had indirect lighting. The lower center on the dash contained the knobs and switches with an ashtray on either side of the radio grille. The steering wheel sported a unique *Tear-Drop* shaped horn button and half circle horn ring. New for this year, sealed beam headlamps.

The big surprise for 1940 was the introduction of the Ambassador Special Cabriolet designed by Alexis de Sakhnoffsky. It weighed 150 pounds less than the stock convertible and purported to do 95-100 mph, twenty were built but only eleven were actually sold. The remainder of unsold units were converted back to stock convertibles. Over-all, convertibles continued to be the low production cars with 206 of the Ambassador Sixes and 93 of the Eights being built.

On sales of $73,489,574. the company made a profit of $1.5 million, which would have been larger had it not invested in developing an all-new car for 1941, the Ambassador 600. The 600 designation was based on the claim that the car would go 600 miles on a tank of gas.

This would be the last year for the venerable LaFayette series as it would be replaced by the 600 series. The 600 would represent the next generation of Nash cars and would continue on through 1948.

1939

The Ambassador Six, *"Slipstream"* 4-door sedan, pictured here with movie actress and Hollywood celebrity, Constance Moore. Optional grille guard and white wall tires.

The Lafayette DeLuxe *"Slipstream"* 4-door sedan, shown bare bones with no options.
Photos courtesy AMC archives

The LaFayette DeLuxe Business Coupe, with optional white wall tires, wheel trim rings and front bumper over-rider grille guard. Extra cargo area was found behind the seats

The smart looking Ambassador Six Convertible Coupe sold for $1,050, only 100 built.

Photos courtesy Yahoo.com Images and The AMC archives

The Ambassador Eight *"Trunk Back"* Sedan with optional white wall tires and rear fender skirts. The new front fender design provided space for the water-fall grille trim.

Squared flush-mounted head lamps were incorporated into the newly designed front fenders. The *"Trunk Back"* sedans provided more cargo space than the *"Slipstream"*. Bumpers were a simple single blade, with two bumper guards in the front and two in the rear. Front center bumper guard and over-rider grille guard are options. <u>Note:</u> The *"Trunk Back"* hinges are mounted on the outside. *"Slipstream"* were mounted inside.

1939 Lafayette

Wheelbase 117.0 inches. Engine: 234.8 cu.in., 6-cylinder in-line, 99 hp.

Model	Price	Built
DeLuxe 4-dr Sedan T/B+	$865.	
DeLuxe 4-dr Sedan F/B*	855.	
DeLuxe 2-dr Sedan	855.	
DeLuxe Bus Cpe 3-p	825.	
DeLuxe Cvt All-Purpose 5p	950.	} Total Built
DeLuxe Cpe All-Purpose 5p	860.	37,302
Special 4-dr Sedan F/B*	840.	
Special 2-dr Sedan	810.	
Special 4-dr Sedan T/B+	840.	
Special Bus Cpe 3p	770.	

1939 Ambassador Six

Wheelbase 121.0 inches. Engine: 234.8 cu. in., 6-cylinder in-line 105hp

Model	Price	Built
Sedan 4-dr T/B+	$ 985.	3,900
Sedan 2-dr F/B*	955.	402
Cpe 5p	960.	350
Cvt Cpe 5p	1,050.	100
Bus Cpe 3p	925.	213
Sedan 4-dr F/B*	985.	3,535

1939 Ambassador Eight

Wheelbase 125.0 inches, Engine: 260.8 cu.in., 8-cylinder in-line 115hp

Sedan 4-dr T/B+	$1,235.	1,910
Sedan 2-dr F/B*	1,205.	69
Cpe 5p	1,210.	118
Cvt Cpe 5p	1,295	34
Bus Cpe 3p	1,175.	63
Sedan 4-dr F/B*	1,235.	1,305

*Indicates *Fast Back (Slipstream) model.*
+Indicates *Trunk Back* model

Information from Encyclopedia of American Cars by Editors of Consumers Guide and Collectible Automobile
April 2005

1940

The Ambassador Convertibles were attractive, but did not sell very well. Only 206 of the Sixes and 93 of the Eights were built. Shown here with optional white walls, front over-rider bars, fog lights and spotlight. Opera seats for two rear passengers. The trunk provided a large cargo area. Deck lid hinges were mounted inside. Front and

rear bumpers were a single blade with two bumper guards front and rear. New for this year, sealed beam headlamps with parking lights mounted in the bezels.

Photos from Yahoo.com Images

The Ambassador Special Cabriolet designed by Alexis de Sakhnoffsky, 20 were built, but only 11 were sold. The remaining were converted back to stock convertibles.

Nash Motors factory executives view the new Ambassador Eight Business Coupe.

Photos courtesy AMC archives

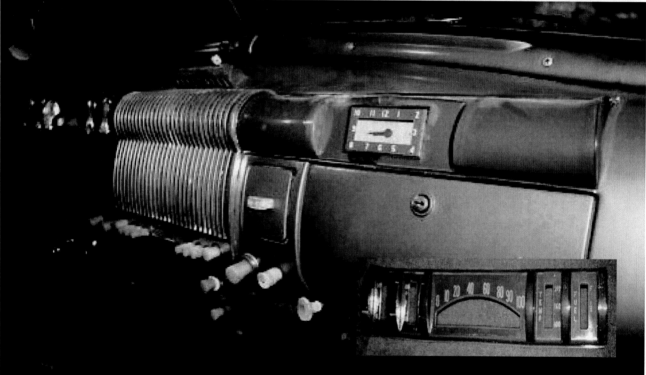

The dash was clean and symmetrical, with all the knobs and switches centered below the radio grille. An optional clock was located in a plastic cut-out above the glove box.

Photos courtesy Yahoo.com Images

The Ambassador Eight 4-dr *"Trunk Back"* Sedan, with optional white wall tires, wheel trim rings and front bumper center guard with over-rider grille guard.

(left to right) Dog dish hub caps standard, trim rings optional. License plate light and trunk lock separate units. Head lamp bezel included parking light. **(top right)** 1939 bumper guards had accent ridges on top, 1940 the ridges were at the bottom.

Photos from Yahoo.com Images.

1940 Nash factory Promo photos demonstrating the unique optional *"Convertible Bed"*

Promoting the *"Weather-Eye"* conditioned air system. It led the industry for 20 years.

1940 LaFayette

Wheelbase 117.0 inches, Engine: 234.8 cu. in., 6-cylinder in-line 99hp

Model	Price	Built
Sedan 4-drT/B+	$875.	17,748
Sedan 4-dr F/B*	875.	12,369
Sedan 2-dr F/B*	845.	9,670
Convert All-Purpose 5p	975.	200
Cpe All-Purpose 5p	850.	901

1940 Ambassador Six

Wheelbase 121.0 inches, Engine: 234.8 cu. in., 6-cylinder in-line 105hp

Model	Price	Built
Sedan 4-dr T/B+	$ 985.	7,248
Sedan 2-dr F/B*	955.	554
Cpe 5p	960.	516
Convert Cpe 5p	1,085.	206
Bus Cpe 3p	925.	323
Sedan 4-dr F/B*	985.	3,653

1940 Ambassador Eight

Wheelbase 125.0 inches, Engine: 260.8 cu. in., 8-cylinder in-line 115hp

Model	Price	Built
Sedan 4-dr T/B+	$1,195.	2,086
Sedan 2-dr F/B*	1,165.	26
Cpe 5p	1,170.	123
Convert Cpe 5p	1,295.	93**
Bus Cpe 3p	1,135.	44
Sedan 4-dr F/B*	1,195.	878

+Indicates *Trunk Back* models
*Indicates *Fastback (Slipstream)* models
**Includes 20 Ambassador Special Sakhnoffsky Cabriolets

Information from Encyclopedia of American Cars by Editors of Consumers Guide

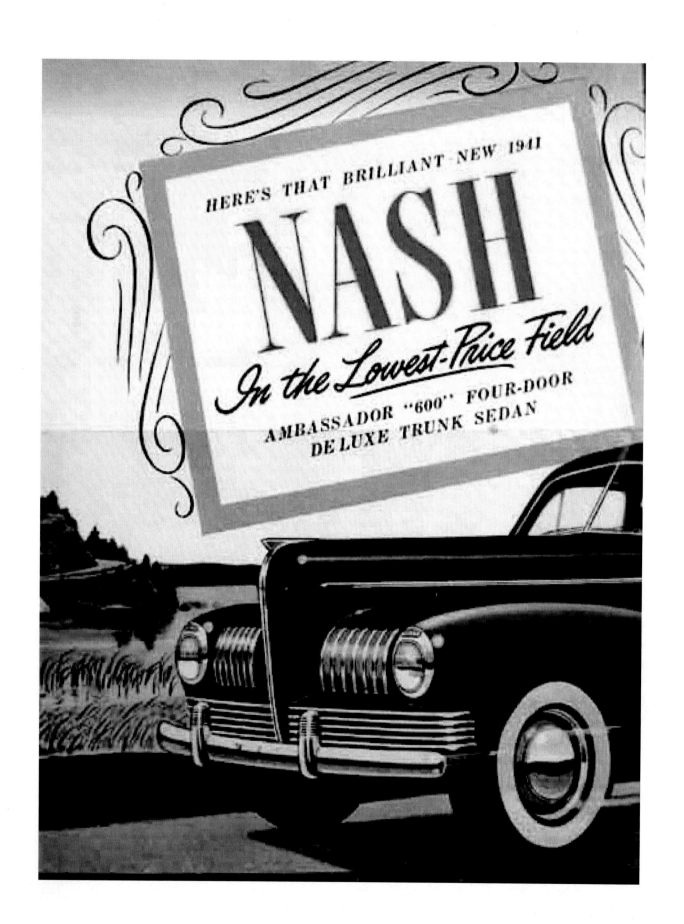

Chapter Two
1941-1942

The big news for 1941 was the introduction of the all new Ambassador 600 series. The 600 designation stood for 600 miles on a tank of gas: 20-gallon tank, 30 mpg. But that wasn't the big news. Unibody was the big news. The 600 was unique being the first production car to use unibody construction. No conventional frame. The unibody construction was developed by Nash engineer/designer Ted Ulrich. Nash became the first automaker to use this type of construction. It is considered standard in the industry today. Structural stampings were welded together to form a rigid unibody, however on the bigger Ambassadors, Nash continued to use a frame.

The 600 series offered 8 models, 5 in the DeLuxe trim and 3 in the Special entry level trim. The 600 had a 112inch wheelbase with a in-line 6-cylinder engine. Offered in the DeLuxe trim; a 4-door *Trunk Back* sedan and a 4-door *Fastback* sedan as well as a *Brougham* 2-door sedan , a *Fastback* 2-door sedan, and a business coupe. In the Special trim, a *Fastback* 4-door sedan, a 5-passenger coupe and a business coupe rounded out the series. *Time Magazine* called the Nash 600 the only completely new car for 1941.

The Ambassador Six series had a 121inch wheelbase powered by a 105hp in-line 6-cylinder engine. The same number of models were offered as the 600, but included a DeLuxe all-purpose Cabriolet (convertible).

The Ambassador Eight series also based on a 121inch wheelbase and powered by a 115hp in-line 8-cylinder engine, with *twin-ignition.* Only five models were offered, including a DeLuxe all-purpose Cabriolet (convertible).

1941 was a profitable year for Nash, earning the company $4.6 million in revenue.

For 1942 Nash offered the same three series with fewer models. An extensive facelift concentrated on the front end, and gave the new model a bolder, stronger, look. The center grille bar stack was broader and shorter. The lower horizontal bars were limited to three, they were wider and continuous across the entire front, and trailed on to the rear of the front fenders. Parking lights were mounted on top of the fenders. Four bumper guards graced the narrow front and rear bumper blades. A handsome winged logo centered above the short grille stack, completed the facelift.

Only five models were offered in the 600 series with a single trim package. The Ambassador Six and Eight series also offered 5 models each with a single trim package. Neither the Ambassador Six or Eight series offered a convertible for 1942. There was no change in engine size from the previous year.

The introduction was met with much enthusiasm and dealers looked forward to a banner year. All this changed with the December 7th attack on Pearl Harbor. Overnight, America was plunged into war. The auto industry responded in kind. All civilian auto production ended on January 30, 1942.

In the shortened model year, Nash managed to produce 37,700 cars, all totaled. With the end of the 1942 model year Nash would no longer offer an 8-cylinder engine. . It would not offer another one until 1955, when the Packard-powered V-8's were introduced.

An interesting side note: as with the rest of the auto industry, cars produced prior to January 1st, 1942, had chrome bright work trim, and models produced after January 1st, known as "Blackout" models, had painted trim. The trim was painted a contrasting color to the body color.

1941

Ambassador Six 4-door F/B Sedan in optional two tone paint scheme. Optional rear fender gravel guards, white wall tires, wheel trim rings and antenna Bright rocker trim molding was standard.

The front end was distinctive, bolder; the horizontal nose bars were gone. The waterfall trim was enhanced and long lower horizontal bars were added.   The grille guard is optional. Trunk hinges on the "*Slipstream" (Fastback)* models were concealed, giving it aerodynamic styling.

Photos from A&E Classic Cars

Ambassador Eight *Brougham* Sedan 5-passenger. Snow plow hood nose less horizontal bars, enhanced waterfall grille trim and added lower wrap around horizontal bars marked the new 1941 front end. Note: parking lights were placed on the top edge of the headlamp bezel.

Ambassador Six 4-door F/B Sedan with optional fog lights, white walls, trim rings and bumper wings.

 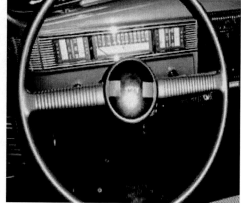

(left) Ambassador Eight dashboard and steering wheel. (right) the Ambassador Six wheel.

Photos from Yahoo.com Images

Richly appointed Ambassador interiors, **(Ambassador Eight above and Ambassador Six below).** Soft Mohairs available in optional colors, *"Billowy"* comfort seating, like your favorite arm chair. Leatherette trimmed lower front seat, carpet trimmed door panels, door to door carpeting, rear assist straps, with coat hooks and built-in arm rests. Wood-grained garnish molding and dashboard. Distinctive steering wheel, door arm rests, left and right, with crank-out vent windows. It all added up to luxury usually found in higher-priced cars.

Photos from A&E Classic Cars. and Yahoo.com Images

The Ambassador Eight *All-Purpose* Cabriolet with optional rear fender skirts, gravel shields front bumper wing guards, spotlight, white wall tires and wheel trim rings.

(left) Ambassador Six 2-dr *Brougham* Sedan. **(right)** Ambassador Six 4-dr T/B Sedan, with optional fender skirts, sun visor, fog lights, white wall tires and bumper wings.

(left) Ambassador Six 4-door T/B Sedan shown in optional two-tone paint. **(right)** the new lower horizontal grille bars were split by vertical nose trim, creating a lower shelf.

Photos from Authors collection and the Internet

32

The 1941 Nash Ambassador 600 2-door *"Fastback"* Sedan. <u>Note:</u> New for this year, the absence of exposed running boards. White wall tires and wheel trim rings are options.

The 600 2-door *"Brougham"* Sedan. White wall tires, wheel trim rings,side view mirrors all popular options. The enclosed, skirt like effect of the rear fender, unique to 600.

(left) The 600 DeLuxe 2-door Brougham. **(right)** The 600 DeLuxe 4-door T/B Sedan.

(left) The 600 Interior front seat. **(upper right)** optional signal-seeking radio with push bar controls. **(lower right)** The Ambassador trunk. Spare was mounted upright at the rear, for maximum cargo area. A full complement of tools was standard. The Ambassador trunk had wall-to-wall carpeting. In contrast, the 600 had a rubber mat.

(left) The 600 series rear fender had a partial wheel cut-out. **(right)** The Ambassador series had a full wheel cut out. The rubber gravel shield was standard. The chrome gravel shield , white wall tires and bright metal wheel trim rings were options.

Photos from Authors collection and Yahoo.com Images

Nash press release photo, promoting the optional rear seat fold down bed conversion.

Nash was supplying the military in 1941 under a defense contract. Shown, 600 Sedan.

Photos from Detroit Public Library and the Internet.

1941 Nash Ambassador 600

Wheelbase: 112.0 inches, Engine: 172.6 cu in, In-Line 6-cylinder, 75hp

Model	Price	Built
Special 4-dr Sedan *Fastback*	$780.	
Special 2-dr Sedan *Fastback*	745.	
Special Bus Cpe 3p	731.	
DeLuxe 4-dr Sedan *Trunk back*	810.	} *
DeLuxe 2-dr Sedan *Fastback*	777.	
DeLuxe 2-dr Brougham 5p	810.	
DeLuxe Bus Cpe 3p	783.	

1941 Nash Ambassador Six

Wheelbase: 121.0 inches, Engine: 234.8 cu in, In-Line 6-cylinder 105hp

Model	Price	Built
Special 4-dr Sedan *Fastback*	$ 970.	
Special 2-dr Sedan *Trunk back*	933.	
Special Bus Cpe 3p	890.	
DeLuxe 4-dr Sedan *Fastback*	1,020.	} *
DeLuxe 4-dr Sedan *Trunk back*	1,065.	
DeLuxe 2-dr Brougham 5p	1,009.	
DeLuxe All-Purpose *Cabriolet*	1,130.	
DeLuxe Bus Cpe 3p	940.	

1941 Nash Ambassador Eight

Wheelbase:121.0 inches, Engine: 260.8 cu in, In-Line Twin Ignition 8-cyl, 115hp

Model	Price	Built
Special 4-dr Sedan *Fastback*	$1,091.	
DeLuxe 4-dr Sedan *Fastback*	1,141.	
DeLuxe 4-dr Sedan *Trunk back*	1,186.	} *
DeLuxe All-Purpose *Cabriolet*	1,130.	
DeLuxe Bus Cpe 3p	940.	

*Total production for 1941, includes all models 84,007

Information from the Encyclopedia of American Cars by Editors of Consumers Guide

Your
NEW 1942 NASH

— here's how to get the maximum
PERFORMANCE, SAFETY *and* **ECONOMY**
that is built into Your car!

1942

(upper) The 1942 Nash Ambassador 600 4-door *"Trunk back"* sedan. The body was unchanged from 1941, but a bolder grille gave the car a whole new look. **(lower left)** The last car off the line on February 1st ,1942 was a 600 2-door Brougham.

Photos from the authors collection, Detroit Public Library, and the Internet.

38

1942 Ambassador Eight Fastback 2door Sedan, shown in optional two-tone paint. Rubber rear fender gravel guards were standard, white wall tires are optional.

The lower grille horizontal bar was carried through the front fender and the rear. Four bumper guards front and rear were standard. Parking lights sat atop the fenders. A chrome accent molding extended from the front of the hood to the back of the trunk.

The 1942 model year was an exercise in contrasts. From Chrome to no chrome, from glitz to somber tones. Chrome trim turned to painted trim in January. It was a reflection of the tense times, it was wartime.

Photos from Yahoo.com images

Photos from authors collection, Nash Archives and the Internet

A REFRIGERATOR AND AN AUTOMOBILE
GO TO WAR !

IT hurtles across the Atlantic between dawn and dinner-time . . . a giant cargo-carrying flying boat with a freight-car load of what it takes to smash an enemy.

This, Mr. Hitler—is a picture of a refrigerator and an automobile *going to war*.

Not by ones or twos—but *in fleets*—these Vought-Sikorskys will soon be sailing from Nash-Kelvinator assembly lines—to fly the fight and might of the U. S. Navy.

And when they stretch their wings around this world, there will be proud new Navy *Corsairs* to protect them—new fighting ships that can fly the wings off any Axis 'plane now known!

The Corsair, too, carries the colors of Nash-Kelvinator. Its powerful 2,000 h.p.

super-charged high-altitude engine is a *quantity* assignment for men who have already built thousands of propellers for the Axis-blasting fliers of the United Nations.

This is just a sample, Mr. Hitler, of our 1943 models. Just a picture of what one company is doing—in meeting and beating a production schedule four times greater than our best peace-time year. And all America's in the fight—buying War Bonds, getting in the scrap metal—in this war *to win!*

So your happy dreams are about over, Adolf—a Nazi nightmare is turning true. The wings of vengeance are coming—from the west!

• • •

NASH-KELVINATOR CORPORATION

NASH **KELVINATOR**

Official civilian car production ended in February, 1942. The auto industry as a whole turned to war production. Nash had supplied the military with vehicles during 1941 and continued with the 1942 models. During World War II Nash built 2000hp engines for fighter planes, precision hydromatic propellers for 18 different types of planes, hundreds of thousands of propeller governors, rocket motors and bomb fuses; cargo trailers and high-powered binoculars for the Army. Nash's five-year war production record was outstanding.

Photos from authors collection and Yahoo.com Images

41

★ Una Carrocería Enteramente Nueva—construida con la solidez de un puente, soldada para formar una sola unidad, más segura, más resistente. A prueba de traqueteo y de torceduras, de una resistencia única.

★ Muelles en Espiral en Las Cuatro Ruedas—una característica exclusiva del Nash entre los coches de más bajo precio—un andar de los más suaves que tiene cualquier marca de automóvil.

Todo Esto

★ Asientos Más Amplios—que los de cualquier otro automóvil. El asiento delantero de los nuevos Nash mide casi metro y medio de ancho. El asiento de atrás es tan ancho que se convierte en cama—la famosa "cama convertible" del Nash Sedan.

★ El Coche Más Fácil de Guiar Del Mundo—El mecanismo de dirección con cojinetes de derecha e izquierda que trae el Nash hace mucho más fácil su manejo en calles transitadas, garajes, etc.

Y además—puede recorrer entre 10 y 12 kilómetros por litro de gasolina

A VELOCIDAD DE CARRETERA.

¡Es un coche enteramente nuevo! Tan grande y tan hermoso — quedará Vd. asombrado cuando sepa lo económico que resulta comprarlo y mantenerlo. Vea hoy mismo este flamante Nash 1942 en el establecimiento de su distribuidor. Tres tipos insuperables de automóviles

Nash—el Nash Ambassador "600", el "6" y el "8".

NASH
Tres Tipos de Automovil Insuperables
DE SEIS Y DE OCHO

1942 Magazine ad in Spanish

1942 Nash Ambassador 600

Wheelbase 112.0 inches, Engine: 172.6 cu in , In-line 6-cylinder 75hp

Model	Price	Built
Sedan 4-door *Trunk back*	$993.	
Sedan 4-door *Fastback*	968.	
Sedan 2-door *Fastback*	948.	} *
Brougham 2-door	958.	
Business Coupe	918.	

1942 Nash Ambassador Six

Wheelbase 121.0 inches, Engine: 234.8 cu in, In-line 6-cylinder 105hp

Model	Price	Built
Sedan 4-door *Trunk back*	$1,069	
Sedan 4-door *Fastback*	1,094.	
Sedan 2-door *Fastback*	1,024.	} *
Brougham 2-door	1,034.	
Business Coupe	994.	

1942 Nash Ambassador Eight

Wheelbase 121.0 inches, Engine: 260.8 cu in, In-line 6-cylinder 115hp

Model	Price	Built
Sedan 4-door *Trunk back*	$1,119.	
Sedan 4-door *Fastback*	1,094.	
Sedan 2-door *Fastback*	1.065.	} *
Brougham 2-door	1,084.	
Business Coupe	1,035.	

* Total Model year production 31,780 ending January 31, 1942

Information from The Encyclopedia of American Cars by Editors of Consumer Guide

Headed for History!

Today, the eyes of the motoring public are on Nash.

For the new Nash "600"—now in production—has basic engineering advances that cars of the future are bound to follow.

With the new Nash "600" you can get 25 to 30 miles on a gallon of gas, at moderate highway speeds! Thousands of extra miles per set of tires.

The Nash "600" is a big car—big in size, big in comfort. It has head-room, leg-room and elbow-room for six big people. It has independent coil springs that never need lubrication—on all four wheels—providing a new kind of ride ... smooth and quiet on any kind of road.

You can drive the Nash "600" in dust, sleet, snow or rain, in comfort. For the Nash conditioned air system delivers in summer a flow of filtered, fresh air ... in winter a draft-free atmosphere of thermostatically-controlled air, with all the windows closed.

You can even have a built-in convertible double bed that turns your car into a camper's dream!

This combination of advances is found today in only one automobile. They are made possible by Nash engineering ... Nash research ... Nash forward-thinking in meeting future demands ... the kind of thinking that tossed out 500 pounds of dead weight and put in its place the single unit of welded steel that is stronger, safer, lighter, forever squeak-proof and rattle-proof. This today is recognized as one of the industry's most important contributions to the automobiles of the future.

And this car—with its fast accelerating, easy-handling, quiet operation—with its new-world beauty and tomorrow's engineering—is actually in the low-price field!

Get in touch with your local Nash dealer. Get the full inside story of the Nash "600" and its famed running mate in the medium-price field, the Nash Ambassador.

Nash Motors
Division of Nash-Kelvinator Corporation, Detroit, Michigan

Tune in Nash-Kelvinator's hit musical program Wednesdays 10:30 p. m., E. S. T. · 9:30 p. m., C. S. T. · 8:30 p. m., M. S. T. · 7:30 p. m., P. S. T. · Columbia Broadcasting System

YOU'LL BE AHEAD WITH Nash

44

Chapter Three
1946

Nash began post World War II production in 1945. The first cars rolled off the assembly line on October 27, 1945, and were designated as 1946 models.

Like the rest of the auto industry, the 1946 Nash models were so called warmed over 1942 models. What this amounted to were slight changes in trim. A new nose emblem replaced the winged "N" and *Nash* block letters. Front fender ribs were removed, bumper guards were reduced to two and the parking lights were re-positioned and made part of the grille fascia. All in all it, was a clean looking front end.

Pent up demand was high and there was no need for re-tooling. Only two series were available, the 600 and the Ambassador, both offered only single trim levels. There were only three models in the 600 series; the *Trunk back* sedan, the *Fastback* sedan and the Brougham. In the Ambassador series, there was a *Trunk back* and *Fastback* sedan, a Brougham and the all new Suburban sedan.

The Suburban sedan was the big news for 1946. A *"Woodie"* patterned after the competitive Chrysler Town and Country sedan of 1941-42. The style was similar, but the production method was completely different. Chrysler built their "Woodie" like a station wagon, whereas Nash applied wood over steel. The Suburban followed the lines of the *Fastback* sedan, including the suicide doors. The slight difference was in the deck lid hinges. The Suburban used exterior hinges from the *Trunk back* sedan.

The Suburban was the highest priced model at $1,929. Only 275 were built. Overall 1946 model year production totaled 72,861.

1946

The Ambassador Suburban "Woodie" sedan. Priced at $1.929. Only 275 built.

The Nash Suburban may have been patterned after the successful Chrysler Town and Country but the production method was completely different. Chrysler built the Town and Country like a station wagon (solid wood construction). The Nash method was to apply wood over steel allowing it to follow the lines of the *Fastback* sedan. Note the use of exterior *Trunk back* hinges.

Photos from AMC Archives, conceptcarz.com and Yahoo Images

The dashboard was of the "Art Deco" design carried over from 1942. Simple, yet striking. Applying wood over steel allowed the design to follow that of the *Fastback*

sedan. The wood components were supplied by Ionia Mfg., Ionia. Michigan, and assembled by The Seaman Body Co., Milwaukee, Wisconsin, division of Nash-Kelvinator

1946 Ambassador *Fastback* 4-door sedan. Priced at $1,469. Total produced: 26,925

1947 Ambassador *Trunk back* 4-door sedan. Priced at $1,511. Total produced: 3,875

Photos from Yahoo.com Images and Flickr.com

The *Trunk back* deck lid had exterior hinges, while the *Fastback* had concealed hinges

In 1942, the parking lights, previously located in the headlamp bezels, were moved to the tops of the fenders. In 1946 through 1948 the parking lights became part of the overall grille design, including incorporating horizontal bars into the new bezel.

1942 **(left)** and 1946 **(right)** Note the removal of the extra trim bar on the rear fender.

Photos from Yahoo.com Images and the authors collection

From 1942 **(top)** to 1948 **(bottom)** the grille changed slightly. From the width of the vertical stack to the relocation of the parking lights, to the thickness of the horizontal bars, it still managed to retain its bold look. The horizontal bars carried to the dash.

Photos from authors collection and Yahoo.com Images

Engine turnings and horizontal bars made up the dash. Steering wheel had half a horn ring. The instruments were easy to read and all control knobs were located below the dashboard.

Interior of the Ambassador *Fastback* sedan featured comfortable chair height seating.

1946 Nash 600

Wheelbase 112.0 inches, Engine: 172.6 cu in, in-line 6-cylinder 82hp

Model	Price	Built
Sedan 4-door *Trunk back*	$1,342.	7,300
Brougham 2-door 5 pass	1,293.	8,500
Sedan 4-door *Fastback*	1,298.	42,300

1946 Nash Ambassador

Wheelbase 121.0 inches, Engine: 234.8 cu in, in-line 6-cylinder 112hp

Model	Price	Built
Sedan 4-door *Trunk back*	$1,511.	3,875
Brougham 2-door 5 pass	1,453.	4,825
Sedan 4-door *Fast back*	1,469.	26,925
Sedan 4-door Suburban	1,929.	275

Price and production information from Encyclopedia of American Cars by the Auto editors of Consumer Guide.

1947

Chapter Four
1947-1948

In 1947 the industry as a whole was plagued with strikes and material shortages. Demand remained high and little was changed. The same two series were offered the 600 and the Ambassador with a single trim package for both. Only the grille was tweaked. At close examination, you could tell a 1947 from a 1946. The horizontal center stack bars were made wider and slightly thicker.

The 600 series offered three models, the *Trunk back* 4 door sedan, the *Fastback* 4 door sedan, which was the best selling model, and the 2 door Brougham. The Ambassador series offered the same three models plus the "Woodie" Suburban sedan. Suburban sales more than doubled for 1947.

There was a price increase for 1947. The 600 series went up an average of eight percent. The Ambassador increased an average of fourteen percent. The highest-priced Nash for 1947 continued to be the Ambassador Suburban sedan.

In spite of the strikes and shortages, Nash managed to produce a total 101,000 units for the model year, which was 7,000 more than 1946.

The big news for 1948 was the re-introduction of a convertible, the Ambassador Custom Cabriolet . Nash last produced a convertible in 1941. It was long overdue. The Custom Cabriolet was the highest-priced Nash for 1948 at $2,345. $106. more than the Ambassador Super Suburban.

Demand was still high in 1948, and a total of 110,000 units were produced for the model year, but the design was wearing thin. The public and dealers were looking for something new; they got it in 1949 with the *"Airflytes"*.

1947

Nash became the Pace Car of the 1947 Indianapolis 500 Race. Nash press release.
Photos from authors collection.

The Bed Conversion package. To accomplish the conversion you pulled the seat bottom forward, swung the seat back up (it was held in place with straps attached to the coat hooks) this gave access to the trunk. A shelf in the trunk above the spare was level with the back seat bottom. You slept with your feet extended into the trunk. This configuration was also handy for hauling extra long cargo.

Ambassador Suburban production peaked in 1947 at 595 units. Priced at $2,227.was the highest priced Nash. It was striking, but offered no utilitarian value. However, the bed conversion option and leather upholstery was appealing to sportsmen.

With wood components manufactured by Ionia Mfg, and assembly by Seaman Body, a Division of Nash, the quality was excellent. Interior upholstered in leather with a leatherette headliner and plywood door trim panels, made for easy maintenance.

Photos from Conceptcarz.com, Yahoo.com Images and Flickr.com

1947 Ambassador Brougham 2 door 5 passenger. Sold for $1,751., and a total of 8,673 were sold. Although an option, white wall tires were not available in early 1947.

The 1947 Brougham was unchanged from 1946, except for the grille, where the horizontal bar stack was made wider and thicker. The driving lights are options.

Ambassador *Fastback* 4-door sedan with optional, two tone paint, white wall tires, trim rings, driving lights, radio, chrome gravel guards and dealer installed side view mirrors.

The 1947 Nash 600 *Fastback* 4-door sedan as exported to the European market.

Photos from Yahoo.com Images and Flickr.com

1947 Nash 600

Wheelbase 112.0 inches, Engine: 6-cylinder In-line 172.6 cu in, 82hp		
Model	Price	Built
Sedan 4-door *Trunk back*	$1,464.	21,500
Sedan 4-door *Fastback*	1,420.	27,000
Brougham 2-door 5 pass	1,415.	12,100

1947 Nash Ambassador

Wheelbase 121.0 inches, Engine: 6-cylinder In-line 234.8 cu in, 112hp		
Model	Price	Built
Sedan 4-door *Trunk back*	$1,809.	15,927
Sedan 4-door *Fastback*	1,767.	14,505
Sedan 4-door Suburban	2,227.	595
Brougham 2-door 5 pass	1,751.	8,673

Information from the Encyclopedia of American Cars by the Editors of Consumers Guide.

1948

Re-introduced in 1948, the convertible was available only in the Ambassador Custom series. Only 1,000 were built, at a price of $2,345. Shown here with spotlight option.

Considered a *Trunk back,* the deck lid hinges were exterior and tail lights were horizontal. Blind rear quarters were still being featured, as did the Plymouth. Ford and Chevrolet both featured quarter windows. <u>Note:</u> The chrome trimmed rear splash pan positioned over the bumper blade, giving the appearance of a two piece bumper.

The Ambassador Custom *Trunk back* Sedan. Shown with optional two tone paint scheme, white wall tires, wheel trim rings, spotlight and the ever popular sun visor.

The grille was changed slightly in 1947 by making the horizontal bars thicker. It was unchanged for 1948, continuing the bold look. The Custom series had a bright trim rocker molding. All *Trunk back* models had exterior deck lid hinges. A single stop light was standard on all models in both series. <u>Note</u>: Chrome trim around the rear window.

Photos from Yahoo.com Images

1948 Nash Business Coupe with optional sun visor. Interior unadorned, but attractive.

(left) The 1948 600 Brougham 2 door. **(right)** The 1948 600 4 door *Trunkback* Sedan.

(right) The 1948 Ambassador Super *Fastback* Sedan. Sun Visor and side view mirrors are options. **(left)** Ambassador Super *Trunk back* Sedan; two tone paint is extra cost option.

Photos from Yahoo.com Images and the authors collection

This wagon reportedly is one of two built for the U.S. Forest Service. It's based on a

1948 Nash 600 Brougham. I do not believe this "Woodie" was a factory built car. It looks too much like a one-off custom, built by an unknown body builder and nicely executed. Note: the front steel roof section of the Brougham has been retained. The hood nose has been DE-chromed and a 1949 Plymouth front bumper added.

Ambassador Custom Ivory-colored steering wheel with Lucite horn button and full horn ring. The dashboard changed from 1947, it no longer had ribs over engine turned bright metal. Optional under dash tissue box, clock and signal seeking radio.

The circular analog gauges were very easy to read. The radio bezel was plastic covered with chrome horizontal bars. The clock, which was an extra cost item, matched the gauges.

Photos from Yahoo.com Images

1948 Nash 600
Wheelbase 112.0 inches, Engine 172.6 cu in In-line 6-cylinder 82 hp

Model	Price	Built
Super 4-door *Trunkback* Sedan	$1,587.	25,103
Super 4-door *Fastback* Sedan	1,874.	14,777
Super 2-door Brougham	1,858.	7,221
Custom 4-door *Trunkback* Sedan	1,776.	25,044
Custom 4-door *Fastback* Sedan	1,732.	332
Custom 2-door Brougham	1,727.	170
DeLuxe Business Coupe	1,478.	925

1948 Nash Ambassador
Wheelbase 121.0 inches, Engine: 234.8 cu in In-line 6-cylinder 112hp

Model	Price	Built
Super 4-door *Trunk back* Sedan	$1,916.	14,248
Super 4 -door *Fastback* Sedan	1,874.	14,777
Super 4-door Suburban	2,239.	130
Super 2-door Brougham	1,858.	7,221
Custom 4-door *Trunk back* Sedan	2,105.	4,102
Custom 4-door *Fastback* Sedan	2,063.	4,143
Custom 2-door Brougham	2,047.	929
Custom Cabriolet convertible	2,345.	1,000

Information from Encyclopedia of American Cars by the Editors of Consumer Guide

Nash

1948 Owner's Manual
Series 4840-4860

NASH MOTORS DIVISION OF NASH-KELVINATOR CORP.

1949 Airflyte Nashes roll off the assembly line, destined for eagerly awaiting dealers.

Potential customers and curiosity seekers filled showrooms on the first day showing.
Photos from AMC archives and authors collection

Chapter Five
1949-1950

Wow!! 1949 was Nash's "wow" year. Tom McCahill the new car guru for Mechanix Illustrated, put it this way: "It's smart to have no fenders, and there are no smarter cars on the road now (1949) than the new Nashes." He said of the Ambassador, "The Ambassador is a magnificent looking automobile, inside and out. This car is remarkably agile and fleet. I don't know of a better dollar-for-dollar value buy in its class than the Ambassador." As to the 600, McCahill said, "The 600 is miles ahead of competitors on two counts - economy and comfort. At average speeds it will give between 25 and 30 miles to a gallon."

The individual most responsible for the all-new Nash *Airflyte* cars for 1949, was Vice President of Engineering, Nils E. Wahlberg. Most of the work done on the production models fell to the team of Chief Engineer Meade Moore and Ted Ulrich. (Urlich was the top uni-body designer). He was the man responsible for the 1941 Nashes and he played a big part in the 1949 models.

For 1949 Nash offered only two basic models. The 4-door sedan and a 2-door sedan. Each series had four trim levels. The *Bed Conversion*, a popular option was reconfigured, by folding the front back rest to meet the rear seat. You no longer had to partially sleep in the trunk. All 1949 models shared the same body. Missing from the 1949 line-up was a convertible and a wagon.

It cost $15 million to put the *Airflyte* into production, a hefty price tag. Nash head George Mason considered it a good investment. He was proved right. The year yielded a profit of $26 million. The *Airflyte* was a resounding success.

There were few changes for 1950. The same two models were offered the 2-door and 4-door. Hydra-Matic automatic transmission was an Ambassador option, along with "Selecto-Lift Starting". You lifted the gear shift lever to engage the starter. Over-drive called, "Automatic Fourth Speed Forward" was an available option on all models. It proved to be a customer favorite. Seat belts, for the first time were an option on all models.

Then there were the name changes: the 600 was now called the *Statesman*, the Super-Lounge interior was now the *Sky-Lounge*, the Brougham was now called the *Club Coupe.*

Two trim levels continued: the Super and Custom plus a single Deluxe Business Coupe. Bumper guards were beefed up,and the rear window was made larger by ten inches.

In April, Nash introduced the Rambler series. It was the first Compact Car offered by an American auto maker. Initially, the Convertible was available followed three months later with a Station Wagon. Only one trim level was available. The convertible was called a Landau. Steel framing surrounded the side windows, and the top moved up and down on tracks set into the top window frames, pulled by cables. It was more like a sunroof than a convertible. The station wagon was a 2-door model. With short production runs, the Rambler sold well: 9,300 convertibles and 1,712 wagons. The success of the Rambler proved once more that CEO George Mason was a visionary.

Both models had a wheel base of 100 inches, and were powered by 172.6 cu in 6-cylinder engine. Both had "Airflyte" unibody construction. The Rambler was kind of a smaller version of the senior Nash. Nash President George Mason expected the Rambler to be a real volume seller, however material shortages and a short run curbed any sizable increase in production. Steel, copper and aluminum were still being regulated by the government, and since this was an entirely new car, there was no track record to fall back on. The government finally granted additional material after Nash had showed that it had spent $20 million dollars to develop the car.

The best seller for 1950 was the Statesman Super 4-door sedan. Over 60,000 were sold. 1950 production topped out at 191,865. On April 18, 1950, a milestone was reached, when the two millionth Nash was produced.

1949

The lines of the 1949 Nash 600 2-door sedan were clean, uncluttered and aerodynamic. The one piece curved windshield was new, adding to lower wind resistance. The Nash *Airflyte* had the lowest wind resistance in the industry at 20.7%, which translated into improved gas mileage, and high speed stability.

The exterior sun visor was optional. Coming or going, the new Nash was striking.

Photos from Yahoo.com Images and AMC archives

The Nash 600 Super 4-door sedan was the best selling model. Wind tunnel testing proved that the aerodynamic design including covered wheel wells, decreased drag and improved mileage. The added accessories, spotlight and fog lights (although popular) increased drag and effected overall fuel consumption.

(left) Aerodynamically clean, right from the factory. **(right)** Wind resistance increased with added options: i.e. Spotlight, Fog Lights, Hood Ornament.

Photos from AMC archives and Jim Feiten collection

The 1949 Nash Ambassador Super 4-door sedan in two tone paint, shown with optional: white wall tires, side view mirrors, radio and flying lady hood ornament.

The Nash Ambassador Super Special 2-door sedan with optional rear window wiper.

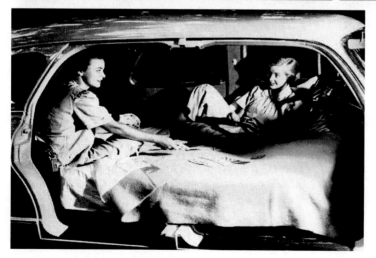

A new bed conversion for 1949. The front seat backs now folded down to meet the back seat, which gave you a larger bed. Your feet no longer stretched into the trunk. A special mattress available

Photos Featuredcars.com and AMC archives

The "Flying Lady" hood ornament was a $9.00 option. It took away the *Airflyte* look.

The new steering wheel included a half horn ring and domed horn button. All the instrument gauges were housed in a pod attached to the steering column. The radio and control knobs were all dashboard mounted. The dashboard design was reminiscent of the Tucker and created a safety well for the front passenger.

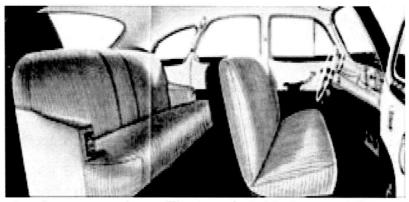

In spite of its narrow opening the trunk was spacious. The comfortable home-style, seating was called the "Super Lounge" interior, upholstered in rich Mohair.

Photos from the AMC archives, Nash Sales Brochure and Yahoo.com Images

1949 4 Door Sedan Ambassador Six
Models 4968 Super
      4998 Super Special
      4978 (Custom)

1949 Brougham (5 Pass.)—2 Door Sedan 6 (Pass.) Ambassador Six
Models 4963 (Super)   4969 (Super)
      4993 (Super Special)   4999 (Super Special)
      4973 (Custom)   4979 (Custom)

1950 4 Door Sedan
Statesman   Ambassador
5048 (Super)   5068 (Super)
5058 (Custom)   5078 (Custom)

1950 Brougham (5 Pass.)—2 Door Sedan Ambassador Six
Models 5063 (Super)   5069 (Super)
      5073 (Custom)   5079 (Custom)

1950 Brougham (5 Pass.)—2 Door Sedan Statesman
Models 5043 (Super)   5049 (Super)
      5053 (Custom)   5059 (Custom)
      5032 (DeLuxe 3 Pass. Business Coupe)

1951 4 Door Sedan
Statesman   Ambassador
5148 (Super)   5068 (Super)
5158 (Custom)   5078 (Custom)

1951 Brougham (5 Pass.)—2 Door Sedan Ambassador Six
Models 5163 (Super)   5169 (Super)
      5173 (Custom)   5179 (Custom)

1951 Brougham (5 Pass.)—2 Door Sedan Statesman
Models 5143 (Super)   5149 (Super)
      5153 (Custom)   5159 (Custom)
      5132 (DeLuxe 3 Pass. Business Coupe)

1949 Nash 600

Wheelbase 112.0 inches Engine: 172.8 cu in, In-line 6-cylinder, 82 hp

Model	Price	Built
Super Special 4-door sedan	$1,848.	2,664
Super Special 2-door sedan	1,824.	9,605
Super Special Brougham	1,846.	2,564
Super 4-door sedan	1,811.	31,194
Super 2-door sedan	1,786.	17,006
Custom 4-door sedan	2,000.	199
Custom 2-door sedan	1,975.	29
Custom Brougham	1,997.	17

1949 Ambassador

Wheelbase 121.0 inches Engine: 234.8 cu in, In-line 6-cylinder, 112hp

Model	Price	Built
Super Special 4-door sedan	$2,243.	6,777
Super Special 2-door sedan	2,218.	2,072
Super Special Brougham	2,239.	807
Super 4-door sedan	2,195.	17,960
Super 2-door sedan	2,170.	4,602
Super Brougham	2,191.	1,541
Custom 4-door sedan	2,363.	6,539
Custom 2-door sedan	2,338.	691
Custom Brougham	2,359.	1,837

Information from Encyclopedia of American Cars by Editors of Consumers Guide

1950

The 1950 Rambler convertible filled the void left in the 1949 line-up. With *Airflyte* construction it proved to be very popular. It was priced at $1,808 and 9,330 were built.

The Rambler was a smaller version of the larger Nash in styling and construction. Promoted as adult seating for five it gave the illusion of being a much larger car.

Photos from AMC archives, Detroit Public Library

The 1950 Rambler station wagon. The "Baby Nash" was America's first "Compact" car. Introduced mid-way through the model year 1,712 were built, priced at $1,808.

A variation on the Station Wagon was the "Deliveryman" which provided a lot of utility for a compact car. Price and number built is unknown. Check the add-on roof rack.

Photos from AMC archives, Detroit Public Library

The 1950 Nash Statesman Super 4-door sedan was the most popular model sold. The side molding, accents the aerodynamic body lines. Because of the lack of a front wheel opening, potential customers often had the salesman demonstrate how to remove the front wheel. A total of 60,080 were built and priced at $1,738., FOB Kenosha, Wisconsin.

Shown here without options. Pure aerodynamic styling made for optimal fuel economy.

Photos courtesy Barrett-Jackson auctions.

The 1950 Statesman Club Coupe (Brougham) shown in two-tone paint scheme with optional sun-visor, fog lights and flying lady hood ornament (a $9.00 option) **(Below)** With its unique rear arm chair seating it was still rated as having seating for five, three in the front and two in the rear. A total of 1,489 were built, priced at $1735.

Photos from Yahoo.com Images Steve Mathews

The 1950 Ambassador Super 4-door sedan. <u>Note:</u> The optional rear window wiper, back-up lights, bumper corner over-rider guards and flying lady hood ornament. Compare the overall aerodynamic styling to the similar Packard pictured in front.

Photos from Yahoo.com Images

1950 Nash Rambler

Wheelbase 100.0 inches, Engine: 172.6 cu in, In-line 6-cylinder, 82hp

Model	Price	Built
Custom Landau Convertible	$1,808.	9,300
Custom 2-door wagon	1,808.	1,712

1950 Nash Statesman

Wheelbase 112.0 inches, Engine: 184.0 cu in, In-line 6-cylinder 85

Model	Price	Built
DeLuxe Business coupe	$1,633.	1,198
Super 4-door sedan	1,738.	60,090
Super 2-door sedan	1,713.	34,196
Super Club Coupe (Brougham)	1,735.	1,489
Custom 4-door sedan	1,897.	11,500
Custom 2-door sedan	1,872.	2,693

1950 Nash Ambassador

Wheelbase 121.0 inches, Engine: 234.8 cu in, In-Line 6-cylinder 115hp

Model	Price	Built
Super 4-door sedan	$2,064.	27,523
Super 2-door sedan	2,039.	7,237
Super Club Coupe (Brougham)	2,060.	716
Custom 4-door sedan	2,223.	12,427
Custom 2-door sedan	2,198.	1,045
Custom Club Coupe (Brougham)	2,219.	108

Information from Encyclopedia of American Cars by Editors of Consumers Guide

Chapter Six
1951-1952

Body design changed slightly for the senior series in 1951. The rear quarter panels dipped at the belt line, defining a rear fender. Nash called it "Sky-Flow". Buick did in 1950 and Kaiser in 1951. A new grille, some trim and tail lights finished off the tweaking. Inside, the "Uniscope" instrument cluster was gone, replaced by a more conventional dashboard. None of these changes were dramatic.

The Rambler on the other hand remained unchanged. However two new models were added. In addition to the convertible and Custom wagon, a Super Suburban wagon and Custom Country Club Coupe 2-door Hardtop were new for 1951.

Rambler production soared to 68,762 units while the senior series sales declined. The Super Statesman 4-door sedan was still the best selling Nash, but sales fell to 52,000 units, from a 60,000 high in 1950. It was clear that Rambler was taking sales away from the larger cars. America liked the compact car idea. Nash President George Mason once again proved to be right.

Long Intrigued by European styling, George Mason was convinced that a similar design was right for America. The go-ahead was given to Nash engineers and stylists. An experimental car, a small convertible, was built. It was called the "NXI" (Nash Experimental International). The car was shipped around the country during 1950-51. Over 250,000 people viewed the car and were asked to fill out a questionnaire. The results of the survey would determine production.

The big news for 1952 was the addition of Hardtop models to the senior series and the Nash-Healey sports car, which was a collaboration with the UK Healey Company and Nash. The car was built in England, using an Ambassador engine.

1951

Big news for 1951, the addition of a hardtop to the Rambler line-up. The Custom Country Club hardtop coupe sold for $1,968 and a total of 19,317 were produced.

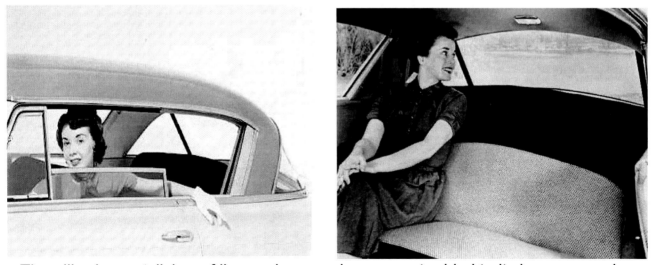

The pillar-less, stylish roof line and an ample rear seat added to its buyer appeal.

Factory Photos from AMC archives

An entry level wagon, the Super Suburban, added to the expanding Rambler series.

The popular Rambler Custom wagon, shown here in two-tone paint with optional flying lady hood ornament. The Nash Weather-Eye system was standard. 19,317 were built.

Factory photos from AMC archives

NASH RAMBLER——Body Style Identification——

1950-52 Rambler Station Wagon
Models 5014 (Super)—5024 (Custom)
5114 (Super)—5124 (Custom)
5214 (Super)—5224 (Custom)

1950-52 Rambler Custom Convertible
Models 5021, 5121 and 5221

1951-52 Rambler Country Club Sedan
Models 5127 and 5227 (Custom)

1953 Rambler Country Club Sedan
Model 5327

1953 Rambler Station Wagon
Models 5314 (Super —5324 (Custom)

1953 Rambler Custom Convertible
Model 5321

The Nash Statesman Super Club Coupe. It sold for $1,952. Only 152 were built. <u>Note</u> the dip in the rear quarter panel belt line was a tweak to the *Airflyte* design.

Cut-away view of the 1951 Nash Statesman Super 4-door sedan. This was the most popular Nash model. It was priced at $1,955. A total of 52,325 were produced.

Photos from AMC Archives and Yahoo.com Images

The Ambassador Custom Club Coupe is one of the rarest of the 1951 models, only 37 were built. The Club Coupes were not popular. You could buy a 2-door sedan for $22. less.

The Ambassador Custom 4-door sedan. This was the last year for the *Fastback.*

Photos from AMC Archives

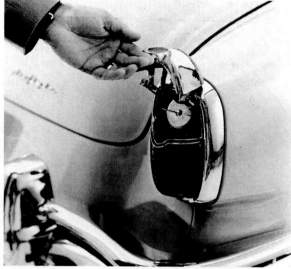

The senior Nash tail light, for 1951 incorporated the gas filler pipe, ala Cadillac.

(left) The Ambassador front bumper and fender spear trim. **(right)** The Statesman front end, less the corner bumper over-rider and the parking light fender spear trim.

Ambassador dash was revamped for 1951. Interior remained comfortably luxurious.

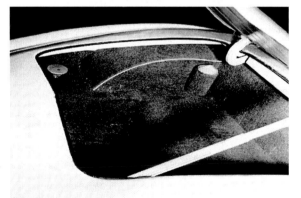

A chance meeting between Donald Healey and George Mason culminated in a joint venture that produced the Nash-Healey; It was America's first production sports car.

Factory photos from AMC archives

Designed by William J. Flojole, the NKI was first introduced at the Chicago Auto Show in 1951**(above).** Nash President George Mason at the wheel checks out the NKI **(below).** It was later renamed the Metropolitan. Built in England by the Austin Motor Company, production began in October 1953. Between 1954-1961, 95,000 were sold.
Factory photos from the AMC Archives

Proposed Pininfarina design for the 1951 Ambassador. The association with the Italian designer began in 1950 and continued through 1956. His influences were prevalent in 1952-54 models,including the Ambassador, Rambler and especially the Nash-Healey.

1951 Nash Rambler

Wheelbase 100.0 inches, Engine: 172.6 cu in, In-Line 6 cylinder 82hp

Model	Price	Built
Super Suburban 2-door wagon	$1,885.	5,568
Custom 2-door wagon	1,993.	28,616
Custom Country Club hardtop	1,968.	19,317
Custom convertible	1,993.	15,259

1951 Nash Statesman

Wheelbase 112.0 inches, Engine: 184.0 cu in, In-Line 6 cylinder 85hp

Model	Price	Built
DeLuxe Business Coupe	$1,841.	52
Super 4-door sedan	1,955.	52,235
Super 2-door sedan	1,928.	22,261
Super Club Coupe	1,952.	152
Custom 4-door sedan	2,125.	18,846
Custom 2-door sedan	2,099.	2,141
Custom Club Coupe	2,122.	38

1951 Nash Ambassador

Wheelbase 121.0 inches, Engine: 234.8 cu in, In-Line 6 cylinder 115hp

Model	Price	Built
Super 4-door sedan	$2,330.	34,935
Super 2-door sedan	2,304.	4,382
Super Club Coupe	2,326.	40
Custom 4-door sedan	2,501.	21,071
Custom 2-door sedan	2,474.	1,118
Custom Club Coupe	2,496.	37

Information from the Encyclopedia of American Cars by Editors of Consumers Guide

1952

Nash Ambassador Custom Country Club, pillar-less hardtop, was a new model for 1952. It was the highest priced at $2,829. A total of 1,228 were produced. The big styling change for 1952 was the conventional style trunk and wraparound Rambler type rear window, a Pinin Farina design influence. All the *Fastback* models were gone.

The 1952 Nash Statesman Custom Country Club 2-door Hardtop. Priced at $2,433.

Photos from AMC achieves

The Ambassador Custom 2-door sedan with optional white walls, sold for $2,695.

The Statesman Super 2-door sedan, 6,795 were produced. It was priced at $2,144.

Photos from AMC achieves

The Statesman Super 4-door sedan. 1952 best seller. 27,304 were built, priced $2,178.

The Ambassador Super 4-door Pinin Farina edition. With sun-visor and fender skirts.

Photos from Yahoo.com Images and the Internet.

The Custom Country Club hardtop was a big seller for 1952, over 25,000 were built.

Convertible sales were down for the year. Priced at $2,119, only 3,108 were produced. New for 1952 was a stylized hood ornament, which still remained an extra-cost option.

Photos from AMC Archives and Yahoo Images

(left) The Rambler Greenbriar wagon. **(right)** The Rambler Super Suburban wagon.

The Rambler Custom 2-door wagon with "woodie" trim around the window frames.

The Rambler Commercial Deliveryman with front seat only. Based on the Suburban, it was priced at $1,772. This was a bare bones utility vehicle. Few options available.

Photos from AMC Archives and John Tranter

99

Styling for the Nash-Healey had been turned over to Pinin Farina of Italy. The rolling chassis was assembled by Healey in England, then shipped to Farina in Italy for final assembly. The move to a Farina design was in keeping with the rest of the Nash Line.

(left) Nash President George Mason at the wheel checks out the new Nash-Healey. Coming or going the sports car was very inviting. The Pinin Farina design is evident.

Photos from AMC Archives

1952 Dealer showroom, featuring the Rambler Convertible and a replica of the first Rambler built by Thomas Jeffery in late 1800s. Nash purchased Jeffery Motors in 1916.

Photo from Yahoo.com Images

1952 Nash Rambler

Wheelbase 100.0 inches, Engine: 172.6 cu in, In-Line 6 cylinder 82hp

Model	Price	Built
Super Suburban wagon	$2,003.	2,970
Deliveryman wagon	1,772.	1,248
Custom Wagon 2-door	2,119.	19,889
Custom Country Club hardtop	2,094.	25,784
Custom Convertible	2,119.	3,108

1952 Nash Statesman

Wheelbase 114.3 inches, Engine: 195.8 cu in, In-Line 6 cylinder 88hp

Model	Price	Built
Super 4-door sedan	$2,178	27,304
Super 2-door sedan	2,144.	6,795
Custom 4-door sedan	2,332.	13,660
Custom 2-door sedan	2,310.	1,872
Custom Country Club hardtop	2,433.	869

1952 Nash Ambassador

Wheelbase 121.3 inches, Engine: 252.6 cu in In-Line 6 cylinder 120hp

Model	Price	Built
Super 4-door sedan	$2,557.	16,838
Super 2-door sedan	2,521.	1,871
Custom 4-door sedan	2,716.	19,585
Custom 2-door sedan	2,695.	1,178
Custom Country Club hardtop	2,829.	1.228

Information from the Encyclopedia of American Cars by Editors of Consumers Guide

Styled by
PININ FARINA

Nash
Airflyte

AMBASSADOR · STATESMAN

1953
PRESS ·
RADIO · TV
ANNOUNCEMENT

January 15, 1953

Chapter Seven
1953-1954

The Rambler received a much needed face-lift for 1953. The hood was re-worked and now sat below the front fender tops. The heater air intake now extended across the full width of the cowl and the convertible and Country Club Coupe both received a continental spare as standard equipment. These styling changes were the influence of Italian designer Pinin Farina and gave the Rambler a European look. The GM Hydra-Matic automatic transmission was now available on all Rambler models in addition to a manual transmission and over-drive.

Senior Nashes, Statesman and Ambassador received a minor face-lift primarily to the front end: new parking lights and new grille. The Super Statesman 4 door sedan was once again the best selling model. Total 1953 model production amounted to 119,678 units.

Entering 1954 survival was on the mind of Nash President George Mason. Sales had slipped, and he was betting on the Rambler for the new year with three new Rambler models being introduced for 1954. The 2-door sedan in Deluxe and Super trim, The 4-door sedan in Super and Custom trim and the Custom Cross Country wagon. All total, Rambler offered three series and ten models.

The Senior Nashes were unchanged: the Statesman offered five models and the Ambassador only four.

The much heralded Nash Metropolitan went on sale in March 1954. On May 1st, 1954 Nash-Kelventor merged with Hudson Motors to form American Motors. On October 9, 1954, Nash President George W. Mason died. The mantel was passed to George Romney, who became President of the newly-formed American Motors

1953

The Ambassador Custom Country Club 2-door hardtop. The Country Club was also available in the Statesman Custom series. 5,857 were produced for both series.

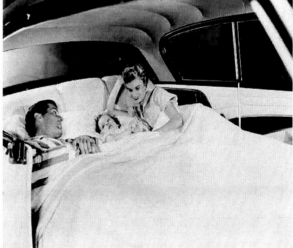

The popular *Sleeper* conversion option was available in the Country Club, as shown.

Photos from the AMC Archives

105

The 1953 Nash Statesman Custom Country Club was priced at $2.423 and sold well.

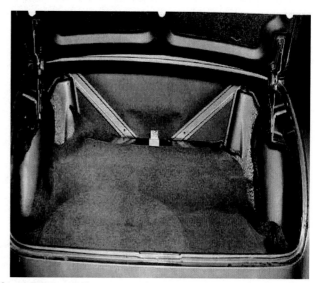

The Senior Nashes received a minor face-lift for1953 and was pretty much unchanged The right tail light hid the gas filler pipe, just like Cadillac. The trunk was very large.

Photos from the AMC Archives and authors collection

The Statesman Super 4-door sedan was the best selling model 11,401 were built.

The Senior model dashboard was new for 1952 and remained unchanged for 1953

Photos from the Detroit Public Libaray

The Statesman Custom 2-door sedan was the least popular model. Only 24 were built. It was priced at $2,310. The Ambassador version fared a little better, with 283 built.

The only change for Senior Nashes in 1953 was to the front end (primarily the grille and parking lights). The optional hood ornament was designed by renowned pin-up artist George Petty, of World War II fame. He was famous for his pin-up girl calendars.

Photos from AMC Archives, Sales Brochure and the Internet

The Rambler Country Club 2-door hardtop. Rambler received a major face-lift. The hood was re-worked and now sat below the front fender tops. The heater intake now extended across the full width of the cowl. Added to this was a continental spare.

New for 1953 was the addition of the continental spare, which provided more trunk capacity. The massive nose emblem of 1951-52 gave way to a Nash logo centered on the grille bar. The Rambler Country Club was available in Super and Custom trim.

Photos from the Detroit Public Libaray

The Greenbriar Custom Station Wagon with two tone accent paint. It was an upgraded version of the the standard Custom wagon. A total of 10,571 were built.

The large nose emblem was replaced with a logo disc centered on the grille bar. The hood ornament continued to be optional The spare sat under under the cargo floor.

The Rambler convertible for 1953 featured a continental spare, which gave it a European look. The Pinin Farina logo emblem was only found on the right front fender.

The Interior was all-vinyl, bold and bright, in keeping with the 1950s styling. Floor carpeting front and rear. The speedometer cluster also housed the instrument gauges. The radio was optional; turn signals were standard. The glove box was actually a drawer. The Manual transmission was standard and Automatic was optional.

Photos from AMC Archives and the Internet

Only three examples of the Rambler DeLuxe 2-door sedan were built in 1953 for pre-production test purposes. It would be introduced as a new model in 1954.

Sales for the "Deliveryman" utility wagon sagged in 1953. Only 9 units were sold.
Photos from AMC Archives

New for 1953 was the Nash-Healey Coupe, shown here as photographed in England.

Only 60 coupes were built. Total Nash-Healey production for 1953 was only 163 units The Nash-Healey Coupe was introduced at the Chicago Auto Show. The coupe could be ordered with a colored keyed top or contrasting color. The car was a pricey $3,982.

Photos from the AMC Archives

113

There were now two Nash-Healey models available; the Roadster and the Hardtop. !953 would be the last year for the Roadster. Total N-H production was 223 units.

The interior of the Roadster and Hardtop Coupe were identical. The Nash-Healey Roadster in LeMans get-up. The racing version was a totally different animal.

Photos from AMC Archives and Conceptcarz.com

Five pre-production NKI (Nash Kelvenator International) were built for testing in 1953.

Photos from AMC Archives

1953 Nash Rambler

Wheelbase 100.0 inches, Engine:184.0 cu in, 6 cylinder 85hp Manual Trans.
Engine: 196.6 cu in, 6 cylinder 90hp Auto Trans.

Model	Price	Built
DeLuxe 2-door sedan	Prototype	3
Deliveryman Utility wagon	Prototype	9
Super Suburban Wagon	$2.003.	1,114
Custom Wagon	2,119.	10,571
Custom Convertible Coupe	2,150.	3,284
Custom Country Club H.T.	2,125.	16,809

1953 Nash Statesman

Wheelbase 114.3 inches, Engine: 195.6 cu in In-Line 6 cylinder 100hp

Model	Price	Built
Super 4-door sedan	$2,178.	28,445
Super 2-door sedan	2,143.	7,999
Custom 4-door sedan	2,332.	11,476
Custom 2-door sedan	2,310.	1,305
Custom Country Club H.T.	2,433.	7,025.

1953 Nash Ambassador

Wheelbase 121.3 inches, Engine: Std. 252.6 cu in, 6 cylinder 120hp.
Engine: Overdrive 252.6 cu in ,6 cylinder 140hp

Model	Price	Built
Super 4-door sedan	$2,557.	12,489
Super 2-door sedan	2,521.	1,273
Custom 4-door sedan	2,716.	12,222
Custom 2-door sedan	2,695.	428
Custom Country Club H.T.	2,829.	6,438

Information from the Encyclopedia of American Cars by Editors of Consumers Guide
and the Standard Catalog of American Cars By John Gunnell

1952 4 Door Sedan

Statesman	Ambassador
5245 (Super)	5265 (Super)
5255 (Custom)	5275 (Custom)

1952 2 Door Club Sedan

Statesman	Ambassador
5246 (Super)	5266 (Super)
5256 (Custom)	5276 (Custom)

1952 Custom 2 Door Country Club
5257 (Statesman)—5277 (Ambassador)

1953 Custom 2 Door Country Club
5357 (Statesman)—5377 (Ambassador)

1953 2 Door Club Sedan

Statesman	Ambassador
5346 (Super)	5366 (Super)
5356 (Custom)	5376 (Custom)

1953 4 Door Sedan

Statesman	Ambassador
5345 (Super)	5365 (Super)
5355 (Custom)	5375 (Custom)

1954

The new Nash Metropolitan introduction, dealer preview, Chicago Auto Show, 1954.

Nash Dealers from around the country eagerly check out the new Metropolitan Hardtop and Convertible. The new car was enthusiastically, unanimously, accepted.

Photos from Detroit Public Library

Best selling author John Brownfield poses with his new 1954 Metropolitan convertible.

European styling of the new Metropolitan. Trunk entry from behind the rear seat back.

Photo from AMC Archives and the Internet

Shortly after the merger, Hudson dealers received the Metropolitan, a re-badged Nash

Photos from AMC Archives

New for 1954, the Rambler Custom 4 door sedan. Priced at $1,985, a total of 7,640 were sold. This model was also available in Super trim at $1,795. and 4,313 were built.

The Pinin Farina Rambler Custom Country Club coupe carried a price tag of $1,950. also available in Super trim at $1,800. Production total for both models, 4,683 units.

Photos from AMC Archives

Both the Convertible and Country Club coupe featured the continental spare. The Custom convertible was losing its popularity. Priced at $1,980. only 221 were built.

New for 1954, the Rambler DeLuxe 2-door sedan. 7,273 were built. Priced at $1,550.

Photos from AMC Archives and Yahoo.com Images

The Rambler Super Suburban 2-door wagon, it was $150. cheaper than the Custom at $1,800. but only 504 sold, as compared to the Custom, which sold 2,202 units.

Take out the back seat, increase the cargo floor, and you have the "Deliveryman".

Factory photos from the Detroit Public Library

The striking new Rambler Custom Cross Country wagon, was received favorably. In its inaugural year it sold a hefty 9,039 units. It was the best selling Rambler model.

The Cross Country wagon featured a roof rack and wood grained accent trim. The addition of roof rack increased the already ample cargo capacity. It would become one of the most popular models produced by American Motors. Priced at $2,080.

Photos from AMC Archives

The Statesman Super 4-door sedan, still the best selling model. 11,401 were built. The sedan was also offered with Custom trim and was available in the longer wheelbase Ambassador, in both Super and Custom trim. All models had continental spare tires.

The 2-door sedan was available as the Statesman Super and Custom, and the top of the line Ambassador, in Super trim only. The Statesman Custom only sold 24 units

The Ambassador Custom Country Club hardtop was outsold by the Rambler version. Rambler sales were climbing, while the Senior Nashes were falling behind. It was a sign of the times. By 1956 the Statesman was down to one model, and by 1957 it was gone and only two Ambassador models were available. Rambler became the mainstay

The Farina influence was still evident in 1954 from the front end to the continental spare. The Ambassador Custom Country Club coupe was priced at $2,735,.a drop of $94 from 1953. It was still the most expensive Nash model. A total of 3,581 were built.

Photos from Yahoo.com Images

This is the last year for the Nash-Healey Sportscar. The only model produced this year was the coupe. The Roadster had been dropped at the end of 1953. During its four year run, only 507 units were sold, including both Roadster and Coupe.

In commemoration of its excellent showing at the Le Mans races, a crossed rally flags emblem was affixed to the trunk lid. New for 1954 was the wraparound rear window.

Photos from AMC Archives and Conceptcarz.com

1954 Nash Rambler

Wheelbase 100.0 Inches (2Dr) 108.0 Inches (4Dr), Engine: 184.0 cu in (2Dr Manual), 6-cylinder 85hp, 195.6 cu in (4Dr Automatic), 6-cylinder 90hp

Model	Price	Built
DeLuxe 2-door sedan	$1,550.	7,273
DeLuxe 4-door sedan		1
Deliveryman utility wagon		56
Super Suburban 2-door wagon	1,800.	504
Super 4-door sedan	1,795.	4,313
Super 2-door sedan	1,700.	300
Custom 4-door sedan	1,965.	7,640
Custom 2-door wagon	1,950.	2,202
Custom Convertible coupe	1,980.	221
Custom Country Club hardtop	1,950.	3,612
Custom Cross Country wagon	2,050.	9,039

1954 Nash Metropolitan

Wheelbase 85.0 inches, Engine: 73.8 cu I, In-Line 4-cylinder 42hp

Model	Price	Built *
Convertible Coupe	$1,469.	*
Coupe 3 passenger	1,445.	*

* Combined total production 11,198

1954 Nash Statesman

Wheelbase 114.3 inches, Engine: 195.6 cu in, In-Line 6-cylinder 110hp

Model	Price	Built
Super 4-door sedan	$2,158.	11,401
Super 2-door sedan	2,110.	1,855
Custom 4-door sedan	2,332.	4,219
Custom 2-door sedan	2,310.	24
Custom Country Club hardtop	2,423.	2,276

1954 Nash Ambassador

Wheelbase 121.3 inches, Engine: 252.6 cu in, In-Line 6-cylinder 130hp

Model	Price	Built
Super 4-door sedan	$2,417.	7,433
Super 2-door sedan	2,365.	283
Custom 4-door sedan	2,600.	10,131
Custom Country Club hardtop	2,735.	3,581

Information from the Encyclopedia of American Cars by Editors of Consumers Guide and the Standard Catalog of American Cars 1946-1975 by John Gunnell

References and Resources

Nash Car Club of America
27 Sunny Drive
Pittsburgh, PA 15236
www.nashcarclub.org

Metropolitan Owners Club of North Amerca
2308 Co. Hwy V
Sun Prarie, WI 53590
www.mocna.us

National Woodie Club
PO Box 6134
Lincoln, NE 68506
www.nationalwoodieclub.com

Encyclopedia of American cars
By Editors of Consumers Guide

Standard Catalog of American Cars 1946-1975
By John Gunnell

Collectible Automobile
June 1993 April 1996 April 2000 June 2002 April 2005
Articles by Patrick Foster

Wickipedia.com

Author's note: several internet sites were also consulted.

About the Author

Don Narus is a nationally recognized auto historian and has written several auto books, starting with "Chrysler's Wonderful Woodie" in 1971. He is retired and splits his time between New Albany, Ohio and Palm Harbor, Florida. While serving in the military, he owned a 1948 Nash 600 sedan. In 1950, Don owned a Rambler Convertible. In 1958 he purchased a Rambler sedan and later, during his first year of retirement, he owned a Nash Metropolitan hardtop. He has a weakness for cars, all kinds of cars.
Author may be contacted at: dlnarus@yahoo.com

The Met was purchased by the author in 1993

This book also available as a download E-Book or in "CD" format in full color. For more information contact: www.newalbanybooks.com

Other Books By Don Narus

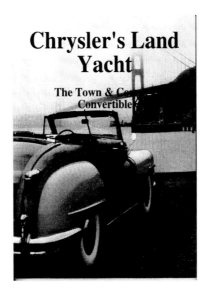

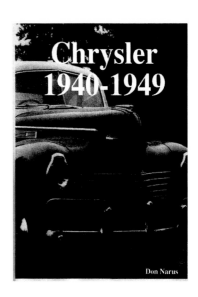

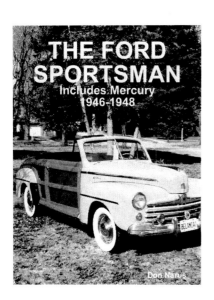

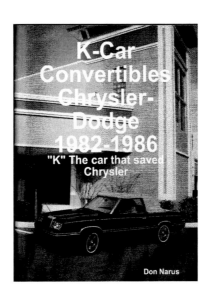

Available from
www.newalbanybooks.com
or www.amazon.com